ENCOURAG

Moms

Member of the
Evangelical Christian
Publishers Association

ENCOURAGEMENT FOR

Moms

BARBOUR
PUBLISHING

"These commands that I give you today are to be upon your hearts. Impress them on your children. Talk about them when you sit at home and when you walk along the road, when you lie down and when you get up."

DEUTERONOMY 6:6–7

A family is a little world created by love.

*M*y mother was an angel on earth.
She was a minister of blessings to all
human beings within her sphere of action.
Her heart was the abode of heavenly purity.

JOHN QUINCY ADAMS

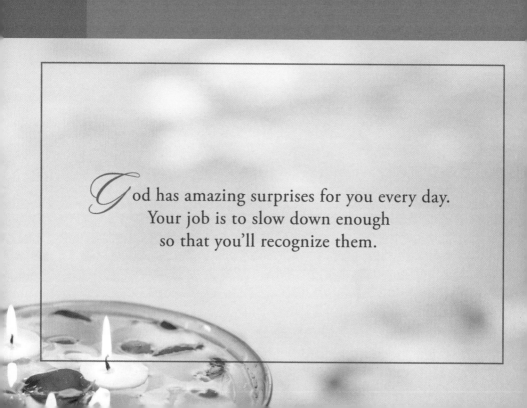

God has amazing surprises for you every day.
Your job is to slow down enough
so that you'll recognize them.

*A mother is one to whom you hurry
when you are troubled.*

EMILY DICKINSON

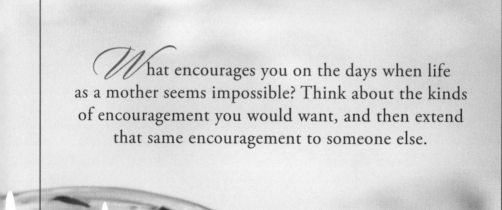

What encourages you on the days when life as a mother seems impossible? Think about the kinds of encouragement you would want, and then extend that same encouragement to someone else.

The truth really will set you free.

There is no place as safe as a mother's arms —
except our Savior's.

*C*hildren and mothers never truly part,
bound in the beating of each other's heart.

CHARLOTTE GRAY

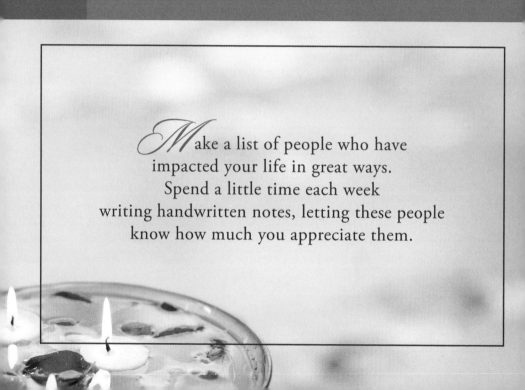

Make a list of people who have
impacted your life in great ways.
Spend a little time each week
writing handwritten notes, letting these people
know how much you appreciate them.

Say to mothers what a holy charge is theirs.
With what a kingly power their love might
rule the fountains of the new-born mind.

L. H. SIGOURNEY

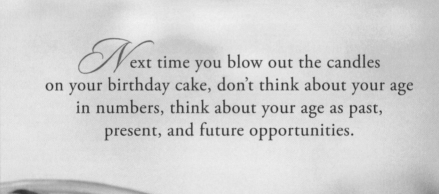

*N*ext time you blow out the candles on your birthday cake, don't think about your age in numbers, think about your age as past, present, and future opportunities.

Pray in lines — at the grocery store,
the bank, or a stoplight —
God would enjoy hearing from you.

A mother's love and prayers and tears are seldom lost on even the most wayward child.

A. E. DAVIS

We can't form our children on our own concepts;
we must take them and love them
as God gives them to us.

JOHANN WOLFGANG VON GOETHE

*R*ead the unfathomable love of those eyes;
the kind anxiety of that tone and look,
however slight your pain.

THOMAS BABINGTON MACAULAY

Mommy was home.
She was the most totally human,
human being that I have ever known;
and so very beautiful.

LEONTYNE PRICE

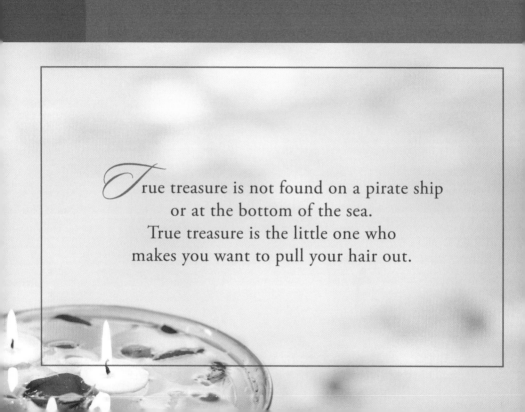

True treasure is not found on a pirate ship
or at the bottom of the sea.
True treasure is the little one who
makes you want to pull your hair out.

A peaceful mother is like a medicinal balm.
Peace and assurance of Mother's love
are necessary ingredients
for a happy home.

WANDA E. BRUNSTETTER

Who ran to help me when I fell,
and would some pretty story tell,
or kiss the place to make it well?
My mother.

ANN TAYLOR

*H*ave planned dates with your children.
If you don't start now, you may look back when
you're old and wonder where the time has gone.

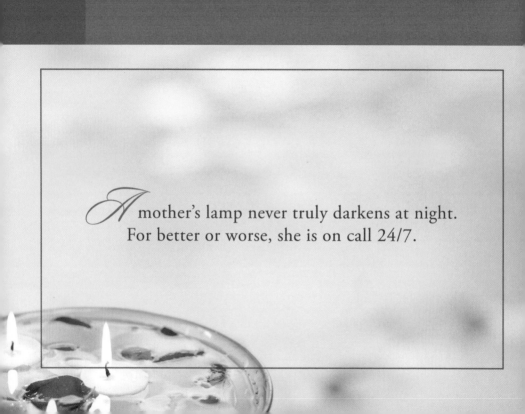

A mother's lamp never truly darkens at night. For better or worse, she is on call 24/7.

Nothing is worth more than this day.

JOHANN WOLFGANG VON GOETHE

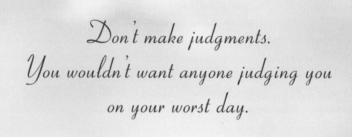

Don't make judgments.
You wouldn't want anyone judging you
on your worst day.

*T*rain your ears to hear not only
your child's cries and giggles,
but your heavenly Father's calling voice.

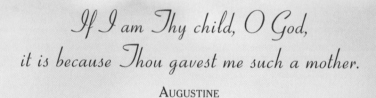

If I am Thy child, O God,
it is because Thou gavest me such a mother.

AUGUSTINE

$\mathcal{D}$issect a mother's heart and see the properties
it doth contain—what pearls of love,
what gems of hope—a mother's heart
beats not in vain.

CALEB DUNN

*T*he Christian home is the Master's workshop where the processes of character and molding are silently, lovingly, faithfully, and successfully carried on.

LORD HOUGHTON

There is a difference
between happiness and joy.
Happiness is a changing emotion.
Joy is a choice you make each day.

Skinned hands and knees
are best healed with a Band-Aid, yes,
but also with soft kisses from Mama.

It is important to ask our children
the question "Why?"
While their younger years are filled
with this pondering question,
we ourselves need to make the time
to understand their perspective, too.

Spend spring planting flowers and watch them grow.
Spend summer enjoying a perfect-temperature pool.
Spend fall playing tag in the forest.
Spend winter making snowballs to throw.

Work to keep your voice soft
and your eyes kind when challenging
another in his or her wrong.

The wolf will live with the lamb,
the leopard will lie down with the goat,
the calf and the lion and the yearling together;
and a little child will lead them.

ISAIAH 11:6

Give your children enough guidance
to lead them in the right direction.
Give yourself enough restraint
to let them become their own people.

$\mathcal{C}$hildren of the heavenly Father
safely in His bosom gather;
nesting bird nor star in heaven
such a refuge e'er was given.

CAROLINA SANDELL BERG

*Ask God for the extraordinary
rather than the ordinary.
He'll give it to you in abundance.*

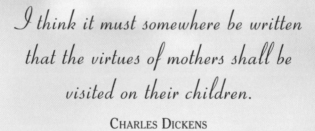

*I think it must somewhere be written
that the virtues of mothers shall be
visited on their children.*

CHARLES DICKENS

Today is a gift and tomorrow is uncertain. Make today—not tomorrow—a day to start working toward what your heart truly desires.

*It's impossible to go through life without needing
to forgive someone or to be forgiven.
Keep the list short and your heart will not ache.*

The happiest moments of my life
have been the few which I have passed
at home in the bosom of my family.

THOMAS JEFFERSON

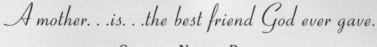

A mother. . .is. . .the best friend God ever gave.

CHRISTIAN NESTELL BOVEE

I want to help you to grow as beautiful
as God meant you to be when
He thought of you first.

GEORGE MACDONALD

Sing throughout the day.
Tone and pitch shouldn't matter.
Sometimes it's even more freeing to sing off-key.

Hugs from children make the makeupless motherhood days just a bit more beautiful.

God provides resting places as well as working places.
Rest, then, and be thankful when
He brings you, wearied, to a wayward well.

L. B. COWMAN

And so we know and rely on the love God has for us.
God is love. Whoever lives in love lives in God,
and God in him. . . . There is no fear in love.
But perfect love drives out fear.

1 JOHN 4:16, 18

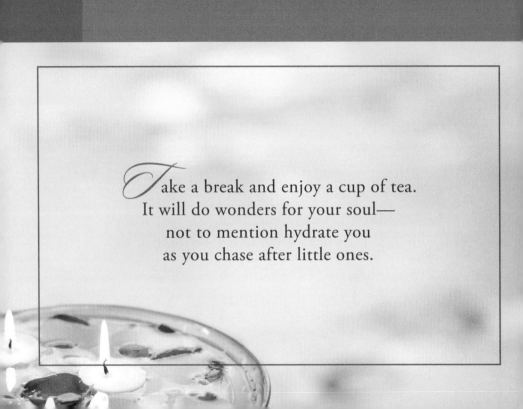

Take a break and enjoy a cup of tea.
It will do wonders for your soul—
not to mention hydrate you
as you chase after little ones.

As long as I live,
I will try to wake each day saying,
"Praise the Lord, it's morning!" not
"Oh, Lord. . .it's morning."

Mother's love grows by giving.

CHARLES LAMB

A child's self-esteem grows when a mother
offers her honest appreciation
and approval of a child's help.

A mother's love has the ability to forgive
even the the most difficult child.

*O*ne of God's richest blessings,
and one of my favorite ironies,
is that our children come into the world
as people we're supposed to guide and direct,
and then God uses them to form us—
if we will only listen.

DENA DYER

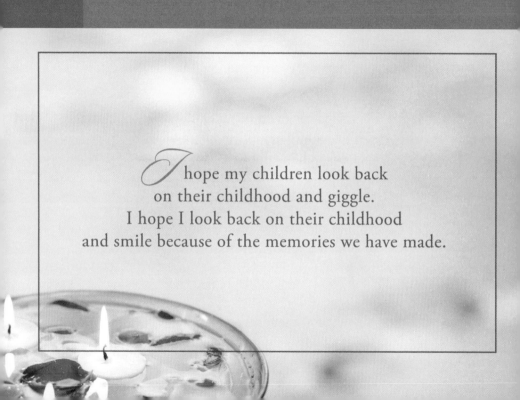

I hope my children look back
on their childhood and giggle.
I hope I look back on their childhood
and smile because of the memories we have made.

There never was a child so lovely but his mother was glad to get him asleep.

RALPH WALDO EMERSON

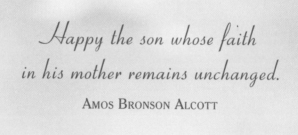

Happy the son whose faith
in his mother remains unchanged.

AMOS BRONSON ALCOTT

*N*o one is useless in this world
who lightens the burdens of it for another.

CHARLES DICKENS

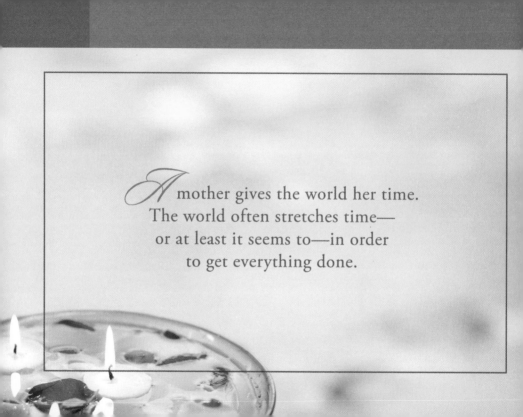

A mother gives the world her time.
The world often stretches time—
or at least it seems to—in order
to get everything done.

Believe that God has a plan for your life.
He sees and loves you.
He desires to know you intimately.

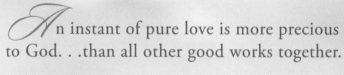

*A*n instant of pure love is more precious
to God. . .than all other good works together.

JOHN OF THE CROSS

Dream in color — you'll sleep better.

One lamp—thy mother's love—amid the stars
shall lift its pure flame changeless,
and before the throne of God,
burn through eternity—Holy—
as it was lit and lent thee here.

NATHANIEL PARKER WILLIS

A family is a unit that no circumstance can truly break.

*M*otherhood:
All love begins and ends there,
roams enough, but having run
the circle, rests at home.

ROBERT BROWNING

It is better to have nobility of character than nobility of birth.

JEWISH PROVERB

*ew activities are nicer than enjoying
a bubble bath and chocolate
after a long, sore day.*

Commit to the Lord whatever you do,
and your plans will succeed.

PROVERBS 16:3

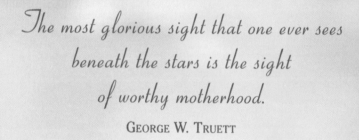

The most glorious sight that one ever sees
beneath the stars is the sight
of worthy motherhood.

GEORGE W. TRUETT

$\mathcal{W}$e are so preciously loved by God
that we cannot even comprehend it.
No created being can ever know how much
and how sweetly and tenderly God loves them.

JULIAN OF NORWICH

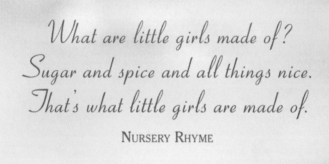

What are little girls made of?
Sugar and spice and all things nice.
That's what little girls are made of.

NURSERY RHYME

*H*e tends his flock like a shepherd:
he gathers the lambs in his arms
and carries them close to his heart;
he gently leads those that have young.

ISAIAH 40:11

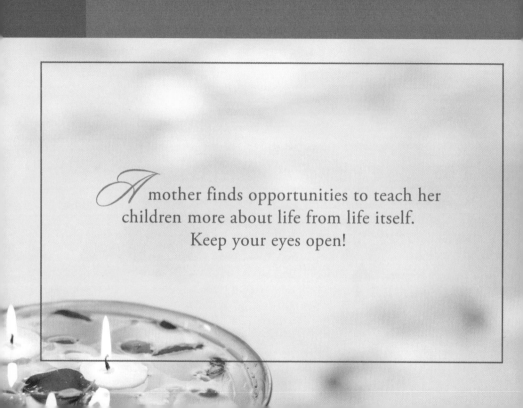

A mother finds opportunities to teach her children more about life from life itself. Keep your eyes open!

We all mold one another's dreams.
We all hold each other's fragile hopes in our hands.
We all touch other's hearts.

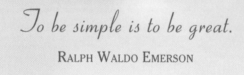

To be simple is to be great.

RALPH WALDO EMERSON

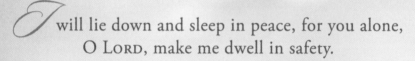

I will lie down and sleep in peace, for you alone, O Lord, make me dwell in safety.

PSALM 4:8

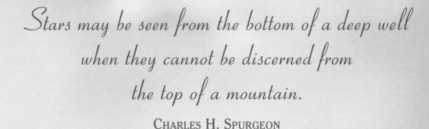

Stars may be seen from the bottom of a deep well when they cannot be discerned from the top of a mountain.

CHARLES H. SPURGEON

*M*ama exhorted her children at every
opportunity to "jump at the sun."
We might not land on the sun,
but at least we would get off the ground.

ZORA NEALE HURSTON

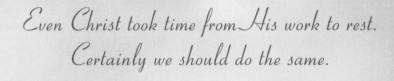

Even Christ took time from His work to rest.
Certainly we should do the same.

*O*nly mothers can think of the future,
because they give birth to it in their children.

MAXIM GORKY

$\mathscr{E}$veryone has a unique role to fill in the world
and is important in some respect.
Everyone, including and perhaps
especially you, is indispensable.

NATHANIEL HAWTHORNE

All that is purest and best in man is but the echo of a mother's benediction.

FREDERICK W. MORTON

ow dear to the heart are the scenes of my childhood, when fond recollection presents them to view.

SAMUEL WOODWORTH

The surest way to be happy
is to seek happiness for others.

MARTIN LUTHER KING JR.

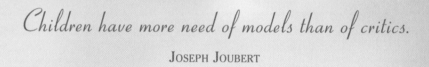

Children have more need of models than of critics.

JOSEPH JOUBERT

*B*eing a full-time mother is one of the highest salaried jobs. . .since the payment is pure love.

MILDRED B. VERMONT

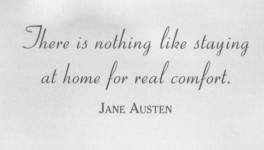

*There is nothing like staying
at home for real comfort.*

JANE AUSTEN

A mother is a person who seeing there
are only four pieces of pie for five people,
promptly announces she never did care for pie.

TENNEVA JORDAN

There is no way to be a perfect mother,
and a million ways to be a good one.

JAN CHURCHILL

Sarah said, "God has brought me laughter."

GENESIS 21:6

*Y*ou have made known to me the path of life;
you will fill me with joy in your presence,
with eternal pleasures at your right hand.

PSALM 16:11

*A mother is not to be compared with
any other person — she is incomparable.*

AFRICAN PROVERB

Then he said to them,
"Whoever welcomes this little child in my name
welcomes me; and whoever welcomes me
welcomes the one who sent me.
For he who is least among you all—he is the greatest."

LUKE 9:48

The most glorious sight that one ever sees beneath the stars is the sight of worthy motherhood.

GEORGE W. TRUETT

A child should always say what's true
and speak when he is spoken to
and behave mannerly at table,
at least as far as he is able.

ROBERT LOUIS STEVENSON

Train a child in the way he should go,
and when he is old he will not turn from it.

PROVERBS 22:6

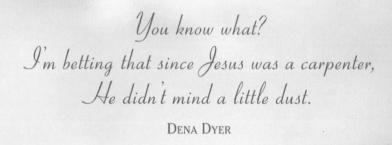

You know what?
I'm betting that since Jesus was a carpenter,
He didn't mind a little dust.

DENA DYER

*S*ometimes I wonder—what kind of example
am I leaving my children?
What will they write on my tombstone
or say about me after I'm gone? . . .
Hopefully my epitaph will read something like this:
"She hated folding laundry but liked
to fold us in her arms."

DENA DYER

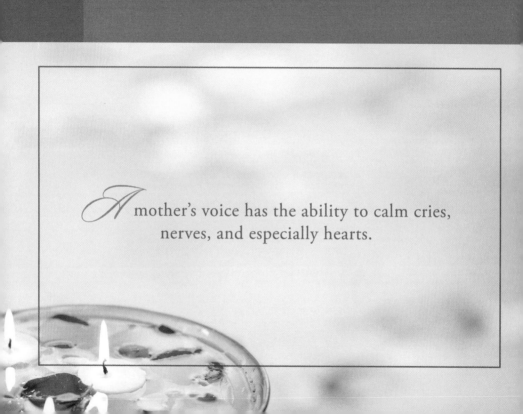

A mother's voice has the ability to calm cries, nerves, and especially hearts.

One good mother is worth a hundred schoolmasters.

GEORGE HERBERT

In every child is the ability to accomplish something great. All they need is a loving push.

$\mathcal{O}$ffering a young child solace in your embrace
is one of the most comforting feelings
in the world—for you, too.

You may have others who will be
more demonstrative but never
who will love you more unselfishly
than your mother or who will be willing
to do or bear more for your good.

CATHERINE BRAMWELL BOOTH

The energy which makes a child hard to manage is the energy which afterward makes him a manager of life.

HENRY WARD BEECHER

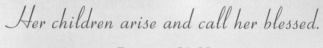

Her children arise and call her blessed.

PROVERBS 31:28

$\mathcal{M}$any wonder why humankind was given
two ears and only one mouth.
The answer, however,
is seen clearly in a mother.

How great the love the Father has lavished on us,
that we should be children of God!
And that is what we are!

1 JOHN 3:1

Use the talents you possess:
The woods would be very silent if no birds
sang there except those that sang best.

One of the amazing ways God lets us become more like Him is through the gift of parenthood.

There is no love on earth, I think, as potent and enduring as a mother's love for her child.

ANN KIEMEL ANDERSON

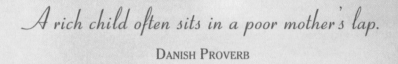

A rich child often sits in a poor mother's lap.

DANISH PROVERB

When a mother is happy,
the whole family is happy.
When a mother is upset,
it might be best for the children to
send themselves to their rooms.

Give a little love to a child
and you get a great deal back.

JOHN RUSKIN

Gentle Jesus, meek and mild,
look upon a little child,
pity my simplicity,
suffer me to come to Thee.

CHARLES WESLEY

He tends his flock like a shepherd:
He gathers the lambs in his arms
and carries them close to his heart;
he gently leads those that have young.

ISAIAH 40:11

The virgin will be with child
and will give birth to a son, and they
will call him "Immanuel" — which means,
"God with us."

MATTHEW 1:23

$\mathcal{G}$ive me Your grace, most loving Jesus,
and I will run after You to the finish line, forever.
Help me, Jesus, because I want to do this
with burning fervor, speedily.

FRANCES XAVIER CABRINI

Love droops; youth fades.
The leaves of friendship fall.
A mother's love outlives them all.

OLIVER WENDELL HOLMES

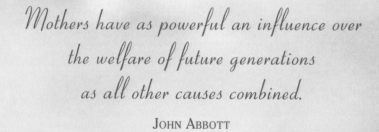

Mothers have as powerful an influence over
the welfare of future generations
as all other causes combined.

JOHN ABBOTT

Jesus said, "Let the little children come to me,
and do not hinder them,
for the kingdom of heaven belongs to such as these."
When he had placed his hands on them,
he went on from there.

MATTHEW 19:14–15

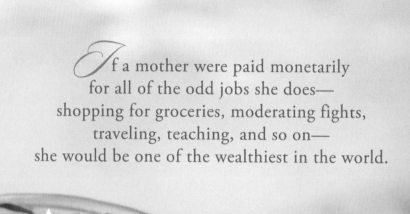

If a mother were paid monetarily
for all of the odd jobs she does—
shopping for groceries, moderating fights,
traveling, teaching, and so on—
she would be one of the wealthiest in the world.

When I approach a child,
he inspires in me two sentiments:
tenderness for what he is,
and respect for what he may become.

LOUIS PASTEUR

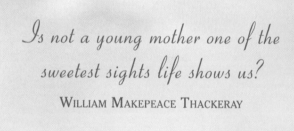

Is not a young mother one of the sweetest sights life shows us?

WILLIAM MAKEPEACE THACKERAY

Trust in the LORD with all your heart
and lean not on your own understanding;
in all your ways acknowledge him,
and he will make your paths straight.

PROVERBS 3:5–6

The babe at first feeds upon the mother's bosom
but is always on her heart.

HENRY WARD BEECHER

I realize I had become a lifelong role model the moment those tiny eyes looked into mine.

UNKNOWN

*A*nybody can build a house;
we need the Lord for the creation of a home.

JOHN HENRY JOWETT

He blesses the home of the righteous.

PROVERBS 3:33

Beneath God's watchful eye
His saints securely dwell;
that hand which bears all nature up
shall guard His children well.

WILLIAM COWPER

*T*hough motherhood is the most important of all the professions—requiring more knowledge than any other department in human affairs—there is no attention given to preparation in this office.

ELIZABETH CADY STANTON

The wisdom that comes from heaven is first of all pure; then peace-loving, considerate, submissive, full of mercy and good fruit, impartial and sincere.

JAMES 3:17

A mother's love always renews itself.

FRENCH PROVERB

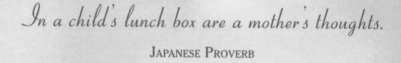

In a child's lunch box are a mother's thoughts.

JAPANESE PROVERB

*I*t is not our exalted feelings;
it is our sentiments that build
the necessary home.

ELIZABETH BOWEN

*G*od's chief desire is to reveal Himself to you
and, in order for Him to do that,
He gives you abundant grace. The Lord gives you
the experience of enjoying His presence. He touches you,
and His touch is so delightful that, more than ever,
you are drawn inwardly to Him.

JEANNE GUYON

*All that I am, or hope to be,
I owe to my angel mother.*

ABRAHAM LINCOLN

Love is patient, love is kind.
It does not envy, it does not boast, it is not proud.
It is not rude, it is not self-seeking,
it is not easily angered, it keeps no record of wrongs.
Love does not delight in evil but rejoices with the truth.
It always protects, always trusts,
always hopes, always perseveres.

1 CORINTHIANS 13:4–7

When you have. . .accomplished your daily task,
go to sleep in peace. God is awake.

VICTOR HUGO

*F*or you know the grace of our Lord Jesus Christ,
that though he was rich,
yet for your sakes he became poor,
so that you through his poverty might become rich.

2 CORINTHIANS 8:9

A mother's love lives on. . . .
She remembers. . .her child's merry laugh,
the joyful shout of her childhood,
the opening promises of her youth.

WASHINGTON IRVING

Train your child in the way in which you know you should have gone yourself.

CHARLES H. SPURGEON

Family relationships are the purest,
cleanest, whitest sand of all.

ROBERT H. BENSON

The mother loves her child most divinely,
not when she surrounds him with comfort
and anticipates his wants, but when she
resolutely holds him to the highest standards
and is content with nothing less than his best.

HAMILTON WRIGHT MABIE

One of the best ways a mother can bless her family is by knowing when to say no and take time for herself.

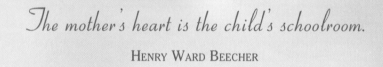

The mother's heart is the child's schoolroom.

HENRY WARD BEECHER

Mild pleasures and palaces though we may roam,
be it ever so humble,
there's no place like home.

JOHN HOWARD PAYNE

May a mother never find herself so busy that she sees herself as being performance-based and not heart-based.

God has given you your child,
that the sight of him,
from time to time, might remind you of
His goodness, and induce you to praise Him
with filial reverence.

CHRISTIAN SCRIVER

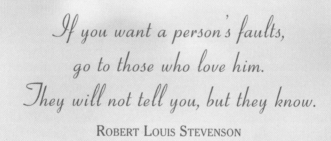

If you want a person's faults,
go to those who love him.
They will not tell you, but they know.

ROBERT LOUIS STEVENSON

*W*e are God's workmanship,
created in Christ Jesus to do good works,
which God prepared in advance for us to do.

EPHESIANS 2:10

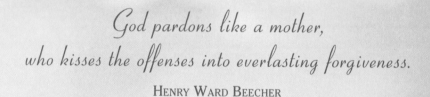

God pardons like a mother,
who kisses the offenses into everlasting forgiveness.

HENRY WARD BEECHER

*M*any waters cannot quench love;
rivers cannot wash it away.
If one were to give all the wealth of his house for love,
it would be utterly scorned.

SONG OF SONGS 8:7

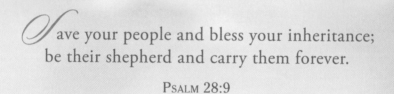

*S*ave your people and bless your inheritance;
be their shepherd and carry them forever.

PSALM 28:9

*To give without any reward, or any notice,
has a special quality of its own.*

ANNE MORROW LINDBERGH

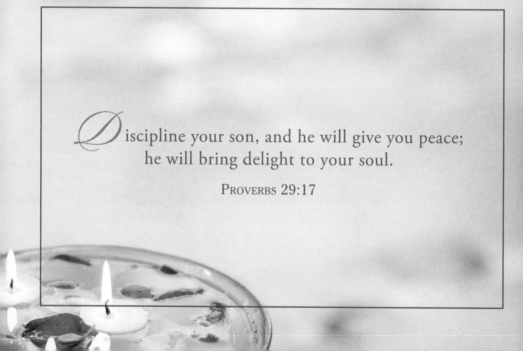

$\mathcal{D}$iscipline your son, and he will give you peace;
he will bring delight to your soul.

PROVERBS 29:17

A mother's patience is like a tube of toothpaste —
it's never quite gone.

UNKNOWN

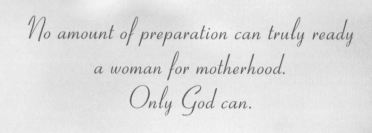

*No amount of preparation can truly ready
a woman for motherhood.
Only God can.*

$\mathscr{B}$lessed is the nation whose God is the LORD,
the people he chose for his inheritance.

PSALM 33:12

My mother said to me,
"If you become a solider, you'll be a general;
if you become a monk, you'll end up as the pope."
Instead, I became a painter and wound up as Picasso.

PABLO PICASSO

Which of all these does not know that
the hand of the LORD has done this?
In his hand is the life of every creature
and the breath of all mankind.

JOB 12:9–10

*M*ay the God of hope fill you with all joy
and peace as you trust in him, so that you may
overflow with hope by the power of the Holy Spirit.

ROMANS 15:13

We remember very little from
our early childhood days.
We should thank God for Mother,
who cared enough to ensure our safety and love.

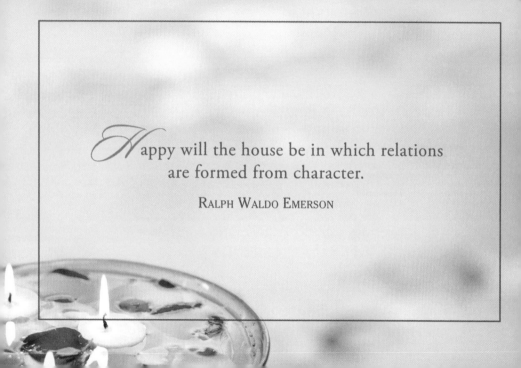

Happy will the house be in which relations
are formed from character.

RALPH WALDO EMERSON

For you created my inmost being;
you knit me together in my mother's womb.

PSALM 139:13

Stories first heard at a mother's knee
are never wholly forgotten—
a little spring that never quite dries up
in our journey through scorching years.

GIOVANNI RUFFINI

Though we lay down our lives for her,
we can never pay the debt we owe
to a Christian mother.

UNKNOWN

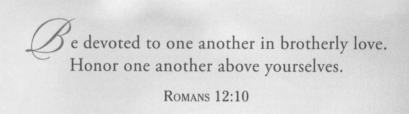

*B*e devoted to one another in brotherly love.
Honor one another above yourselves.

ROMANS 12:10

*The security of the family and family life
are the prime objects of civilization.*

CHARLES ELIOT

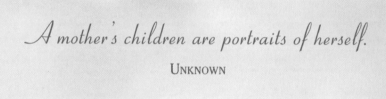

A mother's children are portraits of herself.

UNKNOWN

A new mother should prepare herself
for sleepless nights, prayer-filled days,
and a stirring in her soul that makes her
thankful for every moment spent with her baby.

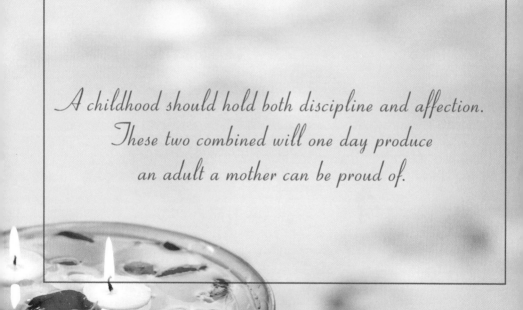

A childhood should hold both discipline and affection.
These two combined will one day produce
an adult a mother can be proud of.

A mother's love for her children
is like nothing else in the world.
It knows no law, no pity; it dares all things
and crushes down remorselessly
all that stands in its path.

AGATHA CHRISTIE

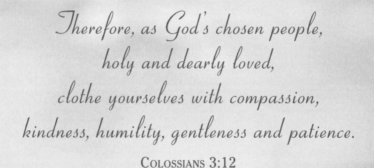

Therefore, as God's chosen people,
holy and dearly loved,
clothe yourselves with compassion,
kindness, humility, gentleness and patience.

COLOSSIANS 3:12

The consciousness of children is formed
by the influences that surround them;
their notions of good and evil are the result
of the moral atmosphere they breathe.

JEAN PAUL RICHTER

*B*lessed are all who fear the LORD,
who walk in his ways.
You will eat the fruit of your labor;
blessings and prosperity will be yours.

PSALM 128:1–2

A child's laughter is more than enough to drown out a tired day in one's soul.

Children are the anchors that hold a mother to life.

SOPHOCLES

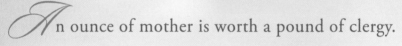

An ounce of mother is worth a pound of clergy.

SPANISH PROVERB

"*For* I know the plans I have for you,"
declares the LORD, "plans to prosper you
and not to harm you,
plans to give you hope and a future."

JEREMIAH 29:11

The house of the righteous contains great treasure.

PROVERBS 15:6

*E*ven though I walk through the valley
of the shadow of death, I will fear no evil,
for you are with me;
your rod and your staff, they comfort me.

PSALM 23:4

Praise the children and they will blossom.

IRISH PROVERB

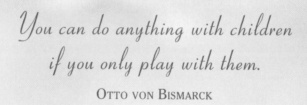

You can do anything with children
if you only play with them.

OTTO VON BISMARCK

*O*nly time will fully tell the impact
of a mother's love, discipline,
and encouragement on her child.

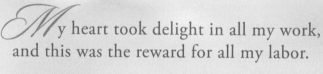

*M*y heart took delight in all my work,
and this was the reward for all my labor.

ECCLESIASTES 2:10

Be patient.
A time will come when your children
will appreciate all that you do for them.

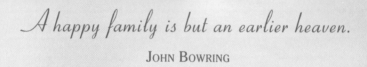

A happy family is but an earlier heaven.

JOHN BOWRING

*H*er dignity consists in being
unknown to the world;
her glory is in the esteem of her husband;
her pleasures in the happiness of her family.

JEAN-JACQUES ROUSSEAU